David Carr Glover
METHOD for PIANO

SIGHT READING and EAR TRAINING

E.L. Lancaster and Gayle Kowalchyk
with David Carr Glover

Sight reading and ear training are two of the most important skills for any musician. Consequently, they should be developed systematically with performance, technical and theory skills from the time that keyboard study begins.

SIGHT READING AND EAR TRAINING, Level Three, correlates with LESSONS, Level Three. As new concepts are introduced in the LESSONS book, they are reinforced visually and aurally in the sight reading and ear training book. SIGHT READING AND EAR TRAINING can be used with equal success in private and group lessons.

The reading exercises in this series are based on the premise that students develop secure reading skills by first playing in specific patterns and gradually moving out of these patterns. The recognition of intervals is crucial to the development of good reading habits. In addition, students must be able to quickly identify individual notes and patterns (melodic, harmonic and rhythmic). Students should practice the assigned reading pages daily and complete any written work on the pages prior to the lesson. At the lesson, the teacher should hear each example.

Note flashes, interval flashes, chord flashes and scale flashes are designed to be used like flashcards. They should be shown rapidly to the student and then covered or taken away to aid in the memory process. Pattern flashes are excerpted from music in the LESSONS book. All of the examples are designed to aid the student in recognizing familiar concepts and executing them at the keyboard.

Listening pages reinforce the concepts being studied from an aural standpoint. They should be completed in the lesson or may be done at home if a parent is able to play the musical examples. It may be necessary to repeat the ear training examples several times for some students. Rhythmic examples that are not notated on the staff should be clapped.

The Teacher's Pages (35-52) contain examples and answers for all of the exercises in the book.

Copyright © 1989 Belwin Mills, c/o CPP/Belwin, Inc., Miami, FL 33014
International Copyright Secured   Made in U.S.A.   All Rights Reserved

Design and Illustrations: Jeannette Aquino
Editor: Carole Flatau

Contents

Supplementary materials correlated with
LESSONS, Level Three, from the
David Carr Glover METHOD for PIANO

Listening REVIEW

1. Listen to I, IV and V7 chords in C major. Identify each chord by writing its Roman numeral name in the blank. The first chord is given.

   a. ___I___ ___ ___ ___   b. ___V7___ ___ ___ ___

   c. ___IV___ ___ ___ ___   d. ___I___ ___ ___ ___

2. Look and listen to melodies using notes from the C major scale. Complete the second and third measures.

   a.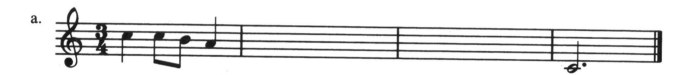

   b.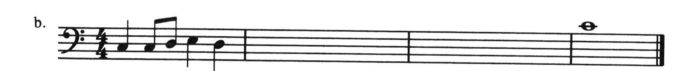

3. Listen to melodic intervals of 4ths, 5ths or 6ths from the C major scale. The bottom note is given. Draw the top note and then play.

   a. 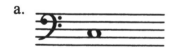   b.    c.

4. Look and listen to the rhythm patterns. Complete the second and third measures using

   ♩. , ♩ , ♩.♪ , ♩ , and ♫ notes.

   a.

   b.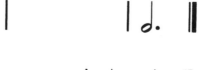

Reading
REVIEW

5. CHORD FLASHES: Write the chord Roman numeral (I, IV or V7) below the chords and then play.

a.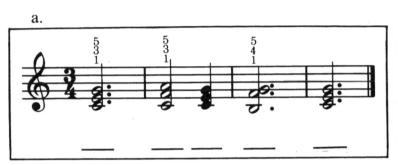

b.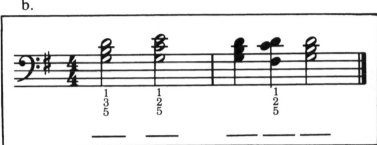

6. PATTERN FLASH: Play and count aloud the pattern.

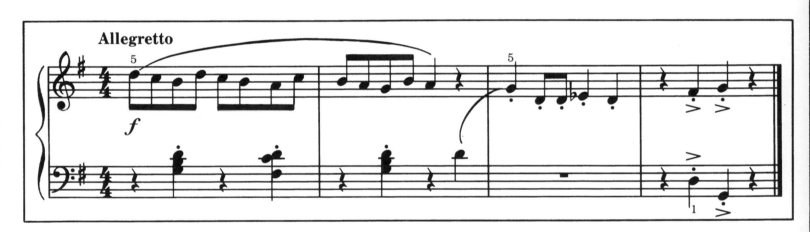

7. READ AND PLAY: Play and count aloud the music. Transpose to C Major.

Use with pages 6-7, LESSONS, Level 3.

Reading
REVIEW

8. SCALE FLASHES: Play and count aloud the scales.

a.

b.

9. PATTERN FLASHES: Play and count aloud the patterns.

a.

b.

10. READ AND PLAY: Play and count aloud the music. Write the chord Roman numeral name on the lines below the bass staff and the chord letter name on the lines above the treble staff. Transpose to G Major.

March tempo

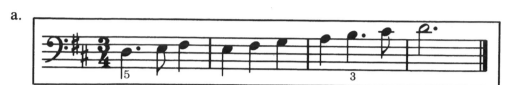

Use with pages 8-9, LESSONS, Level 3.

Listening
REVIEW

11. Circle the chord progression that you hear.

    a. I - IV - I - V7 - I

        I - IV - V7 - V7 - I

    b. I - IV - I - V7 - I

        I - IV - IV - V7 - I

12. Listen to each rhythm pattern. Add a single stem (|) for the quarter and dotted quarter notes, a stem with a flag (♪) for the single eighth notes and stems with a beam (♫) for the two eighth notes.

    a. $\frac{2}{4}$ • • • • | •. • | • • | ♩ ‖

    b. $\frac{3}{4}$ • • • • | • • • | •. • • | ♩. ‖

13. Listen to the intervals. Write H if it is harmonic or M if it is melodic. Name the interval (2nd, 3rd or 4th).

    a. _____ _____   b. _____ _____

    c. _____ _____   d. _____ _____

14. Look and listen to the chords. Add the correct dynamic marking (*f*, *mf* or *mp*) on the lines below the staff.

Reading
LEGER LINE AND SPACE NOTES

15. NOTE FLASHES: Write the name below the note and then play.

a.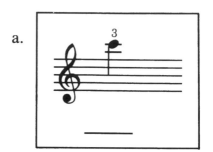

b.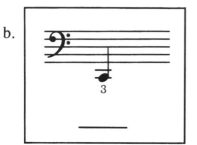

c.

16. INTERVAL FLASHES: Identify the harmonic intervals (3rd, 4th, 5th or 6th) and then play.

a.

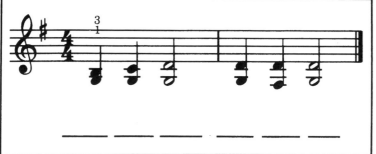

b.

17. READ AND PLAY: Play and count aloud the music.

a.

b.

Use with page 11, LESSONS, Level 3.

Listening
KEY OF C MAJOR

18. Circle the chord progression that you hear.

a.

I   IV   IV   V7   I

b.

I   IV   I   V7   I

I   IV   I   V7   I

I   IV   V7   V7   I

19. Look and listen to the melody. Add an *8va* - - - - - - - - - - - - - ¬ sign above the notes that are played an octave higher than written.

20. Listen to harmonic intervals of 6ths, 7ths or 8ths (octaves) from the C major scale. The bottom note is given. Draw the top note and then play.

a.    b. 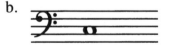   c.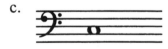

21. Look and listen to each melody. One note will be played incorrectly. Circle the incorrect note.

a.

b.

Use with pages 12-13, LESSONS, Level 3.

Reading
TRIPLETS

22. NOTE FLASHES: Write the name below the note and then play.

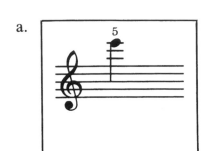 a.

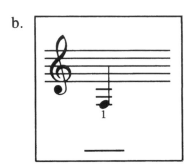 b.

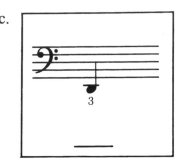 c.

23. PATTERN FLASHES: Play and count aloud the patterns.

a.

b.

24. READ AND PLAY: Play and count aloud the music. Transpose to G Major.

March tempo

Use with pages 14-15, LESSONS, Level 3.

Listening
TRIPLETS

25. Look and listen to the rhythm patterns. Complete the second and third measures using ♩ and 𝄽 .

26. Complete the second measure of the piece using notes from the G major scale and the given rhythm. Play and count aloud.

27. Circle the rhythm pattern that you hear.

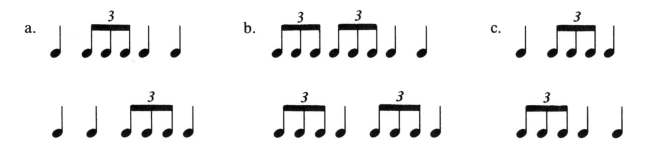

28. Listen to intervals of a 4th or 5th. Circle the correct answer.

a. 4th

    5th

b. 4th

    5th

c. 4th

    5th

Use with pages 16-17, LESSONS, Level 3.

Reading
FIRST INVERSION TRIADS

29. CHORD FLASHES: Write the chord letter name above the first chord in each group and then play.

a.

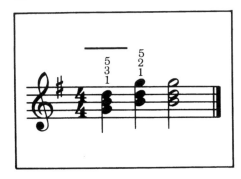

b.

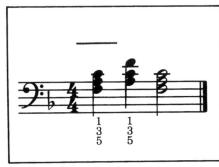

c.

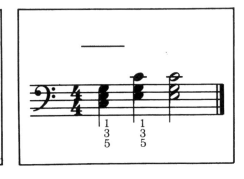

30. PATTERN FLASHES: Play and count aloud the patterns.

a.

b.

31. READ AND PLAY: Play and count aloud the music.

Moderato

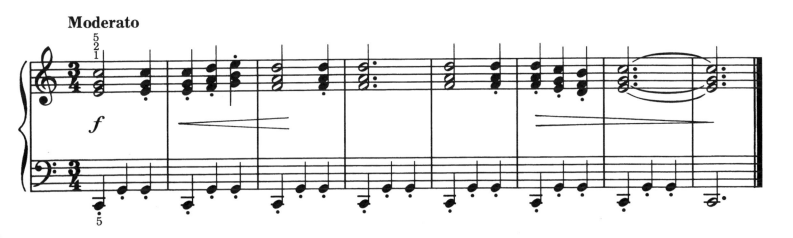

Use with pages 18-19, LESSONS, Level 3.

Listening
FIRST INVERSION TRIADS

32. Listen to major triads in root position and first inversion. Circle the correct answer.

    a.   root position

         first inversion

    b.   root position

         first inversion

    c.   root position

         first inversion

33. Listen to the harmonic major triad in first inversion. Then listen to its notes played melodically. Write the melodic notes in the order that they are played.

    a.

    b.

    c.

34. Circle the chord progression that you hear.

    a.

    b.

    c.

35. Listen to examples in **3/4** and **4/4** meter. Circle the correct answer.

    a. **3/4**   **4/4**   b. **3/4**   **4/4**   c. **3/4**   **4/4**

Use with pages 18-19, LESSONS, Level 3.

Reading
SECOND INVERSION TRIADS

36. CHORD FLASHES: Write the chord letter name above the first chord in each group and then play.

a.

b.

c.

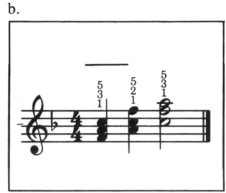
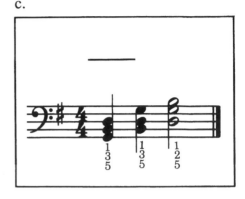

37. PATTERN FLASHES: Play and count aloud the patterns.

a.

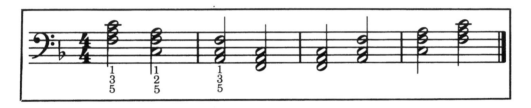

b.

38. READ AND PLAY: Play and count aloud the music. Transpose to D Major.

Use with pages 20-21, LESSONS, Level 3.

Listening
SECOND INVERSION TRIADS

39. Listen to major triads in root position and second inversion. Circle the correct answer.

    a. root position   b. root position   c. root position

        second inversion   second inversion   second inversion

40. Listen to the harmonic major triad in second inversion. Then listen to its notes played melodically. Write the melodic notes in the order that they are played.

41. Circle the chord progression that you hear.

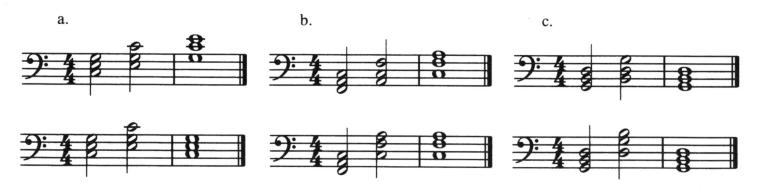

42. Listen to examples in $\frac{2}{4}$ and $\frac{3}{4}$ meter. Circle the correct answer.

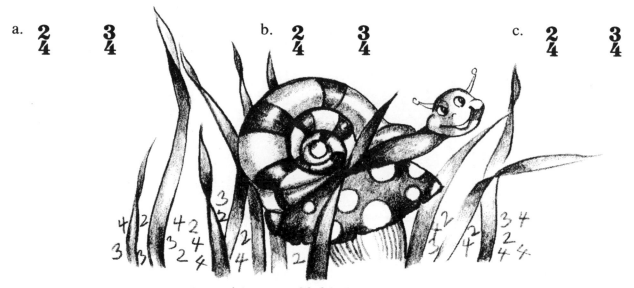

    a. $\frac{2}{4}$ $\frac{3}{4}$ b. $\frac{2}{4}$ $\frac{3}{4}$ c. $\frac{2}{4}$ $\frac{3}{4}$

Use with pages 20-21, LESSONS, Level 3.

Listening
MINOR SCALES

43. Listen to a major or natural minor scale. Circle the correct answer.

    a.   major   b.   major   c.   major

        minor   minor   minor

44. Look and listen to each natural or harmonic minor scale. If it is harmonic minor, raise the 7th tone one half step.

45. Listen to a natural or melodic minor scale. Circle the correct answer.

    a.   natural   b.   natural   c.   natural

        melodic   melodic   melodic

46. Look and listen to the melody using notes from the A harmonic minor scale. Complete the second and third measures.

Use with pages 22-23, LESSONS, Level 3.

Reading
MINOR SCALES

47. SCALE FLASHES: Play and count aloud the scales.

a.

b.

c.

48. PATTERN FLASHES: Play and count aloud the patterns.

a.

b.

49. READ AND PLAY: Play and count aloud the music.

Use with page 24, LESSONS, Level 3.

Listening
MAJOR AND MINOR TRIADS

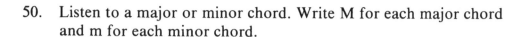

50. Listen to a major or minor chord. Write M for each major chord and m for each minor chord.

    a. _____   b. _____   c. _____   d. _____

51. Listen to the harmonic triad. Then listen to its notes played melodically. Write the melodic notes in the order that they are played.

    a.    b.    c.

52. Listen to major and minor triads. Circle the correct answer.

    a.    b. 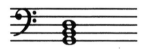   c.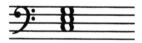

          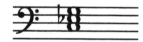

53. Circle the chord progression that you hear.

    a.    b.    c.

Use with page 25, LESSONS, Level 3.

Reading
MAJOR AND MINOR TRIADS

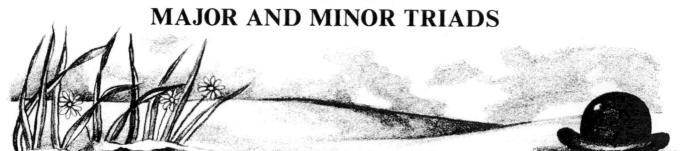

54. CHORD FLASHES: Write the chord letter name above the major or minor chords and then play. Use a small m to indicate minor.

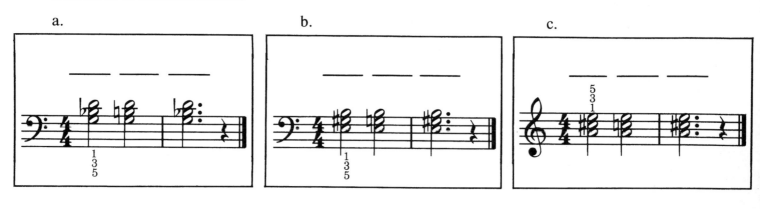

55. PATTERN FLASH: Play and count aloud the pattern.

56. READ AND PLAY: Play and count aloud the music.

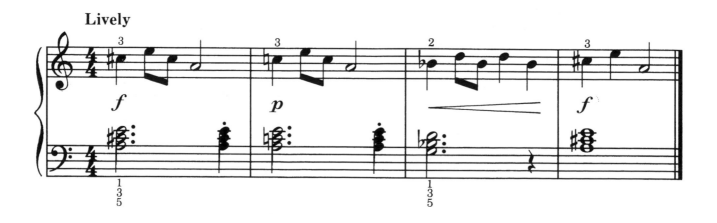

Use with pages 26-27, LESSONS, Level 3.

Listening
PRIMARY CHORDS IN MINOR KEYS

57. Look and listen to each ascending harmonic minor scale. One note will be played incorrectly. Circle the incorrect note.

58. Look and listen to melodies using notes from the A harmonic minor scale. Complete the second and third measures.

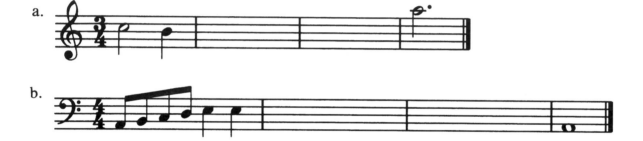

59. Circle the chord progression that you hear.

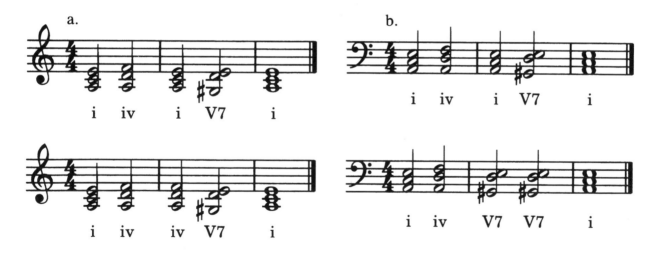

60. Look and listen to the rhythm patterns. Complete the second, third and fourth measures using ♩. , ♩ , ♫♫ , ♩. , ♪ , ♩ and ♫ .

Use with pages 28-29, LESSONS, Level 3.

Reading
PRIMARY CHORDS IN MAJOR AND MINOR KEYS

61. CHORD FLASHES: Write the chord Roman numeral name (I, IV or V7) below the chords and then play.

a.

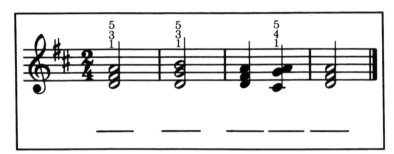

b.

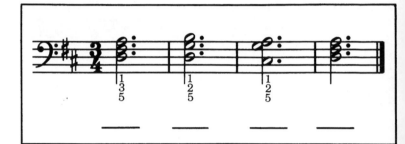

62. PATTERN FLASHES: Play and count aloud the patterns.

a.

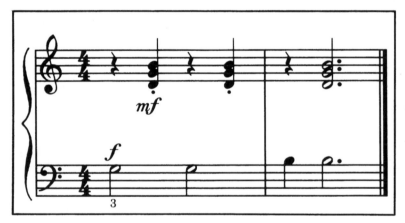

b.

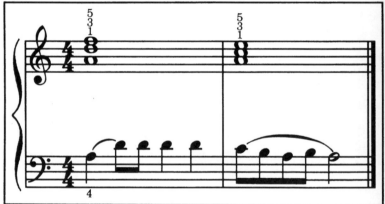

63. READ AND PLAY: Play and count aloud the music.

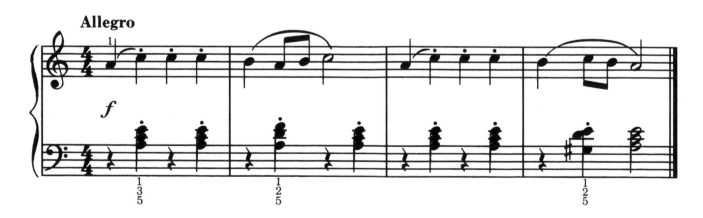

Use with pages 30-31, LESSONS, Level 3.

Listing
PRIMARY CHORDS IN MAJOR AND MINOR KEYS

64. Listen to i, iv and V7 chords in A minor. Identify each chord by writing its Roman numeral name in the blank. The first chord is given.

    a. __i__ _____ _____ _____   b. __i__ _____ _____ _____

    c. __i__ _____ _____ _____   d. __i__ _____ _____ _____

65. Listen to primary chords in major or minor. Circle the correct answer.

    a. major   b. major   c. major

       minor   minor   minor

66. Look and listen to the melody and chords. Identify each chord (i, iv or V7) by writing its Roman numeral name in the blank.

____ ____ ____ ____ ____

67. Look and listen to the music. Add the appropriate musical symbols:

    a. fermata sign (⌢) over the note that is held longer than its original value
    b. ritardando (*rit.*) between the staves when the music begins to get slower
    c. diminuendo sign (⊃═) between the staves in the appropriate place

Use with page 32, LESSONS, Level 3.

Reading
PRIMARY TRIADS AND CHORD INVERSIONS

68. **CHORD FLASHES:** Write the chord letter name above the root position chord in each group and then play.

a.
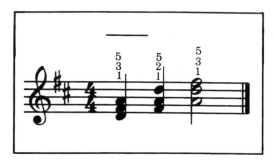

b.
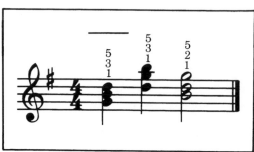

c.
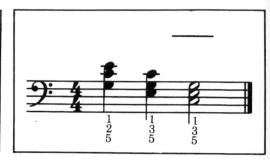

69. **PATTERN FLASHES:** Play and count aloud the patterns.

a.
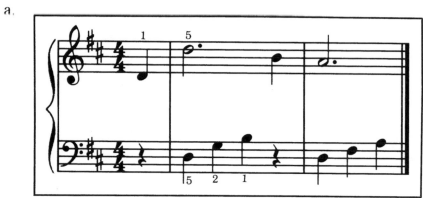

b.
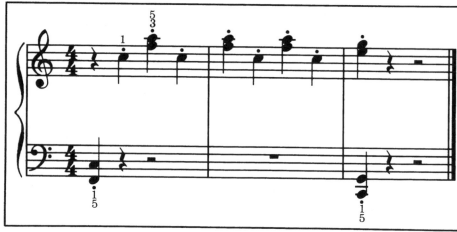

70. **READ AND PLAY:** Play and count aloud the music.

Moderato

Use with page 33, LESSONS, Level 3.

Listening
6/8 TIME SIGNATURE

71. Look and listen to the rhythm patterns. Complete the second and third measures using ♩. , ♫♪ and ♩ ♪ .

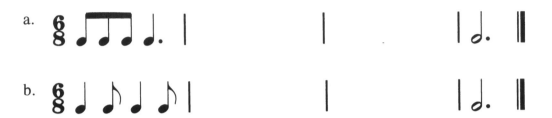

72. Listen to examples in **6/8** and **2/4** meter. Circle the correct answer.

   a. **6/8**   **2/4**   b. **6/8**   **2/4**   c. **6/8**   **2/4**

73. Circle the rhythm pattern that you hear.

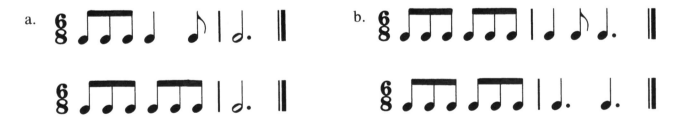

74. Look and listen to the melody and chords. One chord will be played incorrectly. Circle the incorrect chord.

Use with pages 34-35, LESSONS, Level 3.

Reading
6/8 TIME SIGNATURE

75. **CHORD FLASHES:** Write the chord Roman numeral name (i, iv or V7) below the chords and then play.

a.

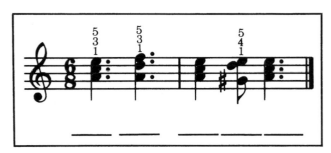

b.

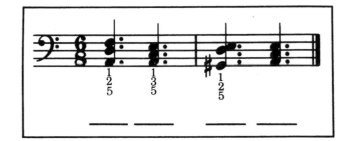

76. **PATTERN FLASHES:** Play and count aloud the patterns.

a.

b.

77. **READ AND PLAY:** Play and count aloud the music.

Allegretto

Use with pages 36-37, LESSONS, Level 3.

Listening
KEY OF D MINOR

78. Look and listen to each natural or harmonic minor scale. If it is harmonic minor, raise the 7th tone one half step.

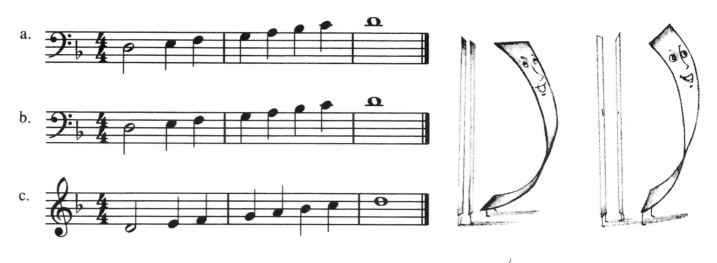

79. Listen to a harmonic or melodic minor scale. Circle the correct answer.

    a.   harmonic   b.   harmonic   c.   harmonic

        melodic   melodic   melodic

80. Look and listen to each ascending harmonic minor scale. One note will be played incorrectly. Circle the incorrect note.

81. Look and listen to the melody using notes from the D harmonic minor scale. Complete the second and third measures.

Use with pages 38-39, LESSONS, Level 3.

Reading
KEY OF D MINOR

82. **CHORD FLASHES:** Write the chord Roman numeral name (i, iv or V7) below the chords and then play.

a.
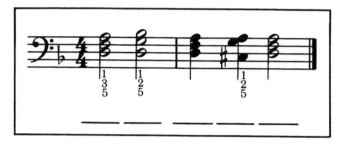

b.
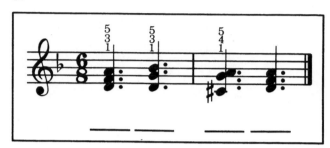

83. **PATTERN FLASHES:** Play and count aloud the patterns.

a.
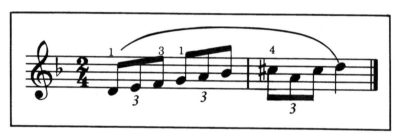

b.
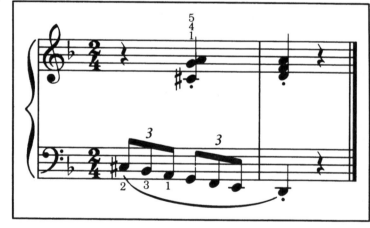

84. **READ AND PLAY:** Play and count aloud the music. Transpose to A minor.

Moderato

Use with pages 40-41, LESSONS, Level 3.

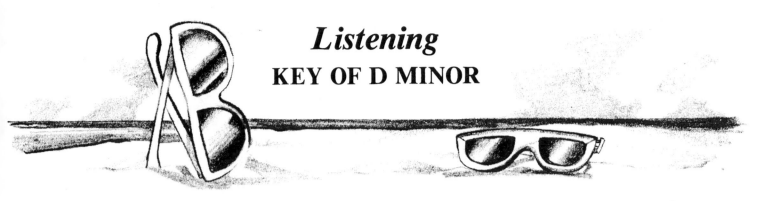

Listening
KEY OF D MINOR

85. Look and listen to the melody and chords. Identify each chord (i, iv or V7) by writing its Roman numeral name in the blank.

_____   _____   _____ _____ _____

86. Circle the chord progression that you hear.

a.

b.

87. Listen to the harmonic triad. Then listen to its notes played melodically. Write the melodic notes in the order that they are played.

a.    b.    c.

88. Circle the chord progression that you hear.

a. i - iv - iv - V7 - i

    i - iv - i - V7 - i

b. i - iv - i - iv - i

    i - iv - i - V7 - i

Use with pages 42-43, LESSONS, Level 3.

Reading
DAMPER PEDAL

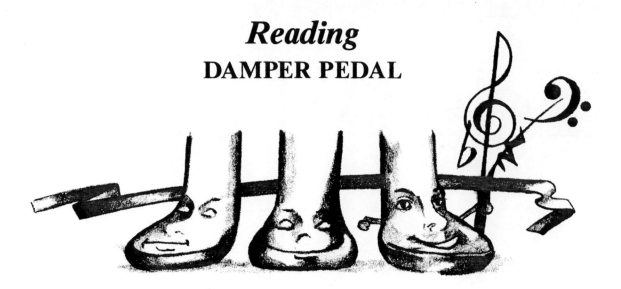

89. CHORD FLASHES: Write the chord Roman numeral name (i, iv or V7) below the chords and then play.

a.

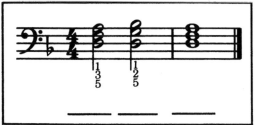

b.

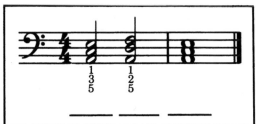

c.

90. PATTERN FLASHES: Play and count aloud the patterns.

a.

b.

91. READ AND PLAY: Play and count aloud the music. Transpose to C Major.

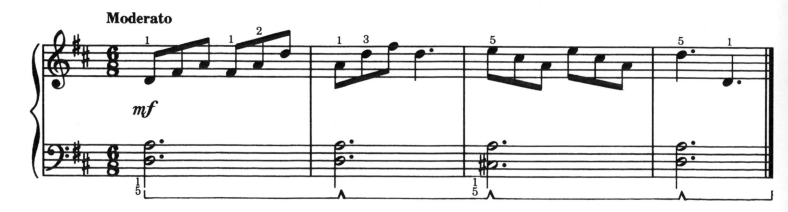

Use with pages 44-45, LESSONS, Level 3.

Listening
SYNCOPATION

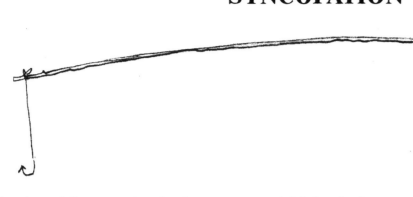

92. Look and listen to the rhythm patterns. Add the tie that you hear.

a.

b.

93. Circle the rhythm pattern that you hear.

a. b. c.

94. Look and listen to the rhythm patterns. Complete the second measure using  or .

a.

b.

95. Listen to a natural or melodic minor scale. Circle the correct answer.

a. natural b. natural c. natural

   melodic melodic melodic

Use with pages 46-47, LESSONS, Level 3.

Reading
SYNCOPATION

96. PATTERN FLASHES: Play and count aloud the patterns.

a.

b.

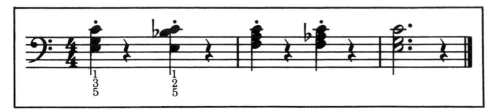

c.

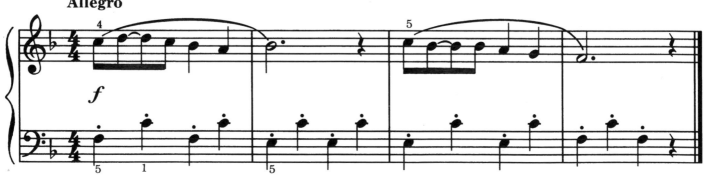

97. READ AND PLAY: Play and count aloud the music.

a.

Allegro

b.

Con brio

Use with pages 48-49, LESSONS, Level 3.

Listening
CHROMATIC SCALE

98. Listen to a major or chromatic scale. Circle the correct answer.

   a. major

   chromatic

   b. major

   chromatic

   c. major

   chromatic

99. Look and listen to the melody using chromatic scale patterns. Complete the second and third measures.

100. Look and listen to the melody and chords. One chord will be played incorrectly. Circle the incorrect chord.

101. Listen to a chromatic or harmonic minor scale. Circle the correct answer.

   a. chromatic

   harmonic

   b. chromatic

   harmonic

   c. chromatic

   harmonic

Use with pages 50-51, LESSONS, Level 3.

Reading
CHROMATIC AND WHOLE TONE SCALES

102. SCALE FLASHES: Play and count aloud the scales.

a.

b.

103. PATTERN FLASHES: Play and count aloud the patterns.

a.   b.

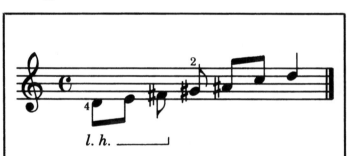

104. READ AND PLAY: Play and count aloud the music.

Use with pages 52-53, LESSONS, Level 3.

Listening
REVIEW

Circle the correct answer.

105. The harmonic interval is a: 4th   5th

106. The melodic interval is a: 6th   7th

107. The major chord progression is: I-IV-I-V7-I   I-IV-V7-V7-I

108. The minor chord progression is: i-iv-i-V7-i   i-iv-iv-V7-i

109. Which rhythm pattern do you hear?   a   b

110. The major triad is: root position   first inversion

111. The major triad is: first inversion   second inversion

112. The minor scale is: harmonic   melodic

113. The minor scale is: natural   harmonic

114. Which rhythm pattern do you hear?   a   b

115. The scale is: chromatic   major

116. Which rhythm pattern do you hear?   a   b

Use with page 54, LESSONS, Level 3.

Reading
REVIEW

READ AND PLAY: Play and count aloud the music.

Use with page 55, LESSONS, Level 3.

Teacher's Pages
SIGHT READING AND EAR TRAINING
Level 3

Student Book Page	Example Number

3

1. a.   b.

   I   V7   V7   I   V7   I   V7   I

c.   d.

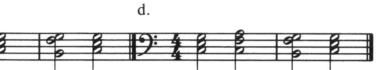

   IV   I   V7   I   I   IV   V7   I

2. a.

b.

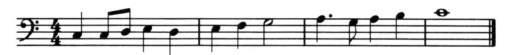

3. a. 6th   b. 4th   c. 5th

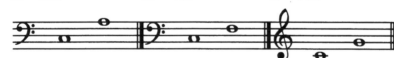

4. a.

b.

4

5. a. I - IV - I - V7 - I   b. I - IV - I - V7 - I

6. PATTERN FLASH: Student plays pattern.

7. READ AND PLAY: Student plays music.

5

8. SCALE FLASHES: Student plays scales.

9. PATTERN FLASHES: Student plays patterns.

10. READ AND PLAY: Student plays music.

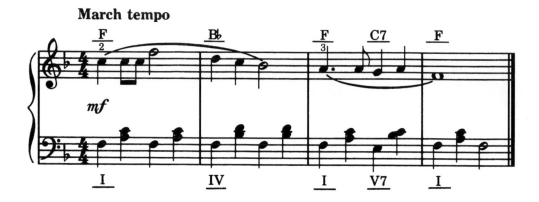

6

11. a.   b.

12. a.

    b.

13. a. M 4th   b. H 2nd   c. H 3rd   d. M 4th

14.

7

15. a. C   b. C   c. F

16. a. 3rd 4th 5th 5th 6th 5th
    b. 5th 6th 5th 4th 3rd

17. READ AND PLAY: Student plays music.

8

18. a.   b.

       I   IV   IV V7   I   I IV   V7 V7   I

19.

20. a. 6th   b. 8th   c. 7th

Teacher Plays:

21. a.

Student Response:

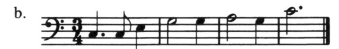

Teacher Plays:

b.

Student Response:

9

22. a. E   b. F   c. D

23. PATTERN FLASHES: Student plays patterns.

24. READ AND PLAY: Student plays music.

10

25. a.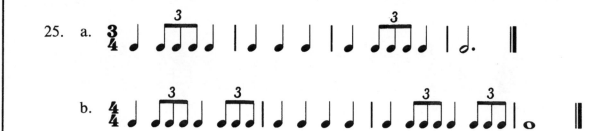

    b.

26.   Student adds notes from G major scale in given rhythm and
plays on keyboard.

27. a.    b.    c.

28. a. 5th   b. 4th   c. 5th

11

29. a. G   b. F   c. C

30.   PATTERN FLASHES: Student plays patterns.

31.   READ AND PLAY: Student plays music.

12

32.

a. root position   b. first inversion   c. first inversion

33. a.   b.   c.

34. a.   b.   c.

12

35. a.

b.

c.

13

36. a. C   b. F   c. G

37. PATTERN FLASHES: Student plays patterns.

38. READ AND PLAY: Student plays music.

14

39. a. second inversion   b. second inversion   c. root position

40. a.   b.   c.

Student Book Page	Example Number

14

41. a.   b.   c.

42. a.

b.

c.

15

43. a. major   b. minor

c. minor

15

44.   a.   harmonic minor   b.   natural minor

       c.   harmonic minor

45.   a.   natural

       b.   melodic

       c.   melodic

46.

16   47.   SCALE FLASHES: Student plays scales.

           48.   PATTERN FLASHES: Student plays patterns.

           49.   READ AND PLAY: Student plays music.

17   50.   a. m   b. m

      c. M   d. m

      51.   a.   b.   c.

      52.   a. minor   b. major   c. minor

      53.   a.   b.   c.

18   54.   a. Gm G Gm   b. E Em E   c. A Am A

      55.   PATTERN FLASH: Student plays pattern.

      56.   READ AND PLAY: Student plays music.

19   57.   Teacher Plays: Student Reponse:
            a.

            b.

19

58. a.

b.

59. a.   b.

i   iv   iv   V7   i   i   iv   i   V7   i

60. a.

b.

20

61. a. I - IV - I - V7 - I   b. I - IV - V7 - I

62. PATTERN FLASHES: Student plays patterns.

63. READ AND PLAY: Student plays music.

21

64. a.   b.

i   iv   iv   i   i   iv   V7   i

c.   d.

i   V7   V7   i   i   iv   i   i

21   65. a. major   b. minor

      c. major

      66.

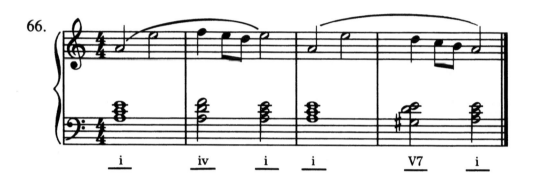

              i   iv   i   i   V7   i

      67.

22   68. a. D   b. G   c. C

      69. PATTERN FLASHES: Student plays patterns.

      70. READ AND PLAY: Student plays music.

23   71. a.

      b.

Student Book Page	Example Number

23

72. a.

b.

c.

73. a.   b.

74. Teacher Plays:

Student Response:

24   75.   a.   i - iv - i - V7 - i   b.   iv - i - V7 - i

      76.   PATTERN FLASHES: Student plays patterns.

      77.   READ AND PLAY: Student plays music.

25   78.   a.   natural minor   b.   harmonic minor

      c.   harmonic minor

      79.   a.   melodic

      b.   harmonic

      c.   melodic

| 25 | 80. | Teacher Plays: | Student Response: |

a.

b.

81.

| 26 | 82. | a. i - iv - i - V7 - i | b. i - iv - V7 - i |

83. PATTERN FLASHES: Student plays patterns.

84. READ AND PLAY: Student plays music.

| 27 | 85.
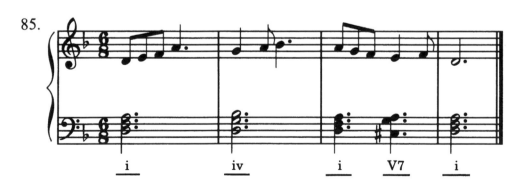

27

86. a.   b.

        i   V7   i   i   iv   V7   i

87. a.   b.   c.

88. a.   b.

      i iv   i V7   i   i iv   i iv   i

28

89. a. i - iv - i   b. i - iv - i   c. i - V7 - i

90. PATTERN FLASHES: Student plays patterns.

91. READ AND PLAY: Student plays music.

29

92. a.

b.

93. a.   b.   c.

94. a.

b.

Student Book Page	Example Number	
29	95.	a. melodic

b. natural

c. melodic

30	96.	PATTERN FLASHES: Student plays patterns.
	97.	READ AND PLAY: Student plays music.
31	98.	a. chromatic

b. major

c. chromatic

31

99.

100.   Teacher Plays:

Student Response:

101.   a.   harmonic

b.   chromatic

c.   harmonic

Student Book Page	Example Number	

32   102.   SCALE FLASHES: Student plays scales.

103.   PATTERN FLASHES: Student plays patterns.

104.   READ AND PLAY: Student plays music.

33   105.   5th

106.   6th

107.

108.

109.   b.

110.   root position

Student Book Page	Example Number	

33

111. first inversion

112. melodic

113. harmonic

114. a.

115. chromatic

116. a.

34

117. - 120.   READ AND PLAY: Student plays music.

FDL01020 $7.95 in US

Alfred

Alfred Publishing Co., Inc.
16320 Roscoe Blvd., Suite 100 • P.O. Box 10003
Van Nuys, CA 91410-0003
alfred.com

ISBN 0-7579-0673-7